Voices of the Earth:
The Future of Our Planet

*A Collection of Original Poetry
and Current List of
Environmental Agencies
in Rhode Island*

Volume 1, No. 2, ©2019
Published by Notable Works
Editor in Chief: Noreen Inglesi, Artist in Residence
Notable Works Publication and Distribution Co., Inc.
Cover Art/Illustrations: Mary Ann Rossoni
Design: Second Story Graphics

table of contents

INTRODUCTION

POETRY

ENVIRONMENTAL AGENCIES

Coalitions

Conservation, Preservation and Restoration

Government Agencies

mission

Notable Works Publication and Distribution Co., Inc. is a 501c3 non-profit corporation founded by Artist in Residence, Noreen Inglesi and Director, Bina Gehres whose mission is to raise awareness for environmental and social concerns through the Arts while providing a venue to local musicians, composers, poets and artists.

publications

Notable Works' Publications Include:

Working In Harmony for Home and Hearth *(2008)*
*A compilation CD project, completed in partnership
with South County Habitat for Humanity,
addressing the issue of homelessness and families
and individuals "in crisis."*

Love Warms the Homeless Heart *(2018)*
*A book of original poetry addressing the issue of
substandard housing and homelessness with a current
listing of shelters and services available in the
state of Rhode Island.*

*For further information please visit
www.notableworks.org*

acknowledgements

Greg Gerritt
*NWF Representative of the
Environmental Council of Rhode Island*

Mary Ann Rossoni
Second Story Graphics

Notable Works' Sponsors and Supporters

Members of the Notable Works' Board of Directors

Members of our Notable Works' Ensemble

Notable Works' Volunteers

CONTRIBUTING

 poets

Aubrey Atwater
atwater-donnelly.com

Elizabeth Bogutt
ebogutt@verizon.net

Nicole DiPaolo
nicolelinadipaolo@gmail.com

David Dragone
crosswindspoetry.com

Dalita Getzoyan
dgetzoyan@gmail.com

Mary Rose His
contact: atwater-donnelly.com

Kelly Melear Hough
kellymhough@gmail.com

Noreen Inglesi
noreeninglesi.com

Thomas Lane
thomaselane@sbcglobal.net

Jan Luby
janluby.com

Karina Lutz
karinalutz.wordpress.com

Peg Paolino
info@notableworks.org

Amybeth Parravano
PeridotRecords.com

Paul Petrie
www.paulpetrie.org

David Riley
davidpriley@aol.com

introduction

We all have different ways of communicating. Essayists describe what they see in prose, poets in poetry, and activists in testimony.

Notable Works has collected Rhode Island poetry of the world around us, the emotions, the sensuality of the living world. They write of warm sunny days, winter nights, and the struggle to maintain a livable planet.

The pairing with a listing of environmental activist groups gives those inspired by the poetry a place to take action, and those engaged in the struggle a place to catch their breath and remember why we do this work.

Greg Gerritt
NWF Representative of the
Environmental Council of Rhode Island

poetry

there's a rift of emerald in the hill

There's a rift of emerald in the hill
Just over yonder
Where the orchards bloom
Past a full moon
And the air's immersed
In the mirth of hummingbirds
There's a rift of emerald
In the hill
Where the weary sky
Stretches and yawns past eventide
Stirring restlessly in the wind
Without ever sleeping
There's a rift of emerald
Where the wounded can heal
In the dazzling myriad
Of monarchs gracefully hovering
With their rainbow wings
There's a rift
Where even the wolves can roam
Unscathed in the untamed night
And where all of Nature
Is lulled to sleep
By the aroma of the
Whispering pines

✺ *Noreen Inglesi*

goosewing beach preserve

At Goosewing Beach a gull
Hoovers high above the searing copper sands
Spreading its wings into the wind
Like a firefly swirling
In the shimmering starlight
It is here that the tern
Can carve its nest in the sands
While the plover gathers bits of broken shells
And tucks itself
Amidst the velvety blanket of the dunes
It is here
That birds
Content with the day's spoil
Can saunter through the ebbing tide
Chasing their reflections into the dawn

※ *Noreen Inglesi*

 *being*

The sun laps at the boat.
The breeze is deep-scented with morning,
all the flowers opening their lives.

Over the gunwales I lean
and watch the bluegills hang
in the cloud-fringed depths,
or dart like thin, grey ripples
under the sky.

I have not come here to fish.
I have come to make my mind
like a still pool,
through which the clouds, the trees, the far blue
hills

may glide

     softly
          as fish.

I prop my head on the thwarts and open my shirt.
The sun glows on my throat
and chest.
      It shines through my skin,
as if my whole body
were glass.

Let the boat drift
wherever the wind wills.

Every shore of the lake is dappled with light
green woods!

❀ *Paul Petrie*

from his book, Rooms of Grace: New and Selected Poems,
New Orleans Poetry Journal Press, 2005

these woods

These woods are fine
These trees, these plants
Chipmunks, crows
Sun, sky, rain, moon
They're fine
The woodland is full of fallen acorns
And I am tripping on a floor of marbles
These woods don't need anything
No clearing, cutting, cleaning, raking
Nothing
They're fine

✺ *Aubrey Atwater*

renewable

The sun glows golden shades on treetops
It's four o'clock
Color is blossoming 'til twilight approaches
Golden haze lights the sky
Calm comes to the earth
Birds fill up 'til morn
Last chance before shadows darken the earth
Twilight leaves
The sun slides beyond to a distant land
The moon shines bright, making paths in the darkness
Day past, night soon gone
The morning sun will awaken
Life will begin again with the new day

Peg Paolino

Lillies rest on the murky pool
while pebbles stir
beneath the minnow swarm.
This is where the sun comes
only once – at noon –
to turn the water into gold
and halt the darkness
of this benign retreat.

The fox creeps here
towards the shaft of warmth.
Weasels and the springing deer
advance, while vireos stop
to sip the sun-filled drink.
At day-time twelve
fear is lost to thirst.

One afternoon I found this place.
How far it was. How lost among
in the greening forest boughs.
The drinking ones had fled
and sun too. No kiss of wind
as I sat to dream and wait.
By the bank of the mute pool.
my mind no longer seemed
on a one way street.

✿ *Mary Rose His*

the tulip

The tulip peeks up from the ground
A tiny, closed bud
Uncertain of how to grow
Or blossom into being

A stranger arrives
With delicate hands providing water, sunlight, care
The tulip takes what she needs to grow
Divine treasures gifted to her
Her instinct is to receive and be nourished

Each day, she is stronger
She grows, grows, grows
What was once a bud
Now a beautiful flower

But her flower is still closed
She wonders, "When will I open?"
"When will I fully blossom?"
"What will I look like?"

One fateful day
The tulip is snipped from her roots
Panic! ensues
Dread fills her being
"That's it," she thinks.
"I will never open, never blossom
Before I wilt away."

The stranger who once cared for her
Thrusts her into the arms of another
The tulip cries in anguish
"No! I need you!
Who will care for me as I die?
Why do you abandon me?"

The tulip looks up at the new stranger
And is surprised to see
The most beautiful smile
Warm, loving
Radiating with delightfully genuine gratitude
She wonders,
"Does this person not know I will soon leave?"

The tulip is brought to a new home
Without roots, without soil
Instead

She is placed on display
For the whole world to see
Her stem
Her flower
Her beauty

She considers the new stranger
Who stands to admire her
Knowing she has not opened up
And knowing she will soon die
"I see what I must do."

With each day, the tulip opens.
She drinks water for comfort
As she painfully blossoms into her full flower
Revealing all to her new friend
Who looks at her with admiration and love

They both know
The more she opens and blooms
The closer she comes to death

The tulip bares all for her friend to see
The friend understands her deeply
The secrets she has been hiding
The beauty she has to offer.

The tulip peaks for another, giving all
Before she wilts away.

✺ *Dalita Getzoyan*

metamorphosis

No greater wonder has e'er unfold
Than the metamorphosis of a butterfly
From a single or cluster of eggs
So carefully sown
Royal succulence concealed in a thick skin
Transformed from unsightly larva
Into a Queen perched atop her throne
Dappled Beauty
Feasting so cozily on the fresh nectar
Of a fully-bloomed orange lily
Flaunting her ivory tipped wings
Resting perhaps from her maiden flight
Brimming with elegance and grandeur
Anxious to share her newly found splendor
By spreading her wings wide
And basking in the soothing winds
Of a gentle summer sky

✾ *Noreen Inglesi*

she's back

Fresh moss and beakfuls of
moist earth
surround the dry relic
of last year's nest
which clings
to the barn

No matter how quietly
I approach
she flits away
silently

Soon it will be time
to hold the pocket mirror
above the nest
and she will patiently stand
on a tree branch,
twitching her tail
until I'm gone

✺ *Aubrey Atwater*

untitled

Ice clings to the falls
in little islands
water rushing around and underneath them
It's only the beginning of official wintertime
there's still January to get through
and February, short on days,
long on loneliness

But for now, December ends...
at 4:30 the darkness descends
the sky holds onto purple-blue
the rest is white, the snow
and grey to black, the trees in silhouette

 And like that little bit of light remaining
I know I won't give up
                    just yet
I'll hold on too...

❀ Jan Luby

untitled

I wanna be an earthworm
I wanna have five hearts
and never find myself
lost on pavement
The winter moon rises orange-gold
so big and low
in the cold, dark, winter sky

And I'm thankful for my eyes
and all my memories of moons
Oh, yes, I will leave them someday
but for now, the moon is mine
and so are all these minutes strung together like pearls,
the clouds of breath in front of my face,
and the sound of my shoes on the sidewalk...

❀ *Jan Luby*

removing bradford dam

Once there was a textile mill
next to a river with a dam
and the river is named Pawcatuck and it stretches for 34 miles
and ends as all rivers must, in the ocean.

The dam was good for the mill
but when the mill closed, the dam was no longer needed
it barricaded the kayaks and the canoes seeking release on the river
and the resident fish and the migrants both
could find no path to their breeding grounds

For over two hundred years the fish in the river
could not swim all the way upstream

When the rains came
the dam would force the river outward
the abandoned mill would be gulping water
and the land surrounding it would drown
in the overflow.

Without a clear pathway,
the shad, the river herring, the trout and others
would swim in circles
their eyes frantically searching for some way forward.

Then scientists and nature lovers who understand that fish
are living creatures, needing to produce more of their own
took the dam down, that dam and other dams
so the river could flow for 34 miles.

The colorful canoes and kayaks now move in symmetry
and the fish can follow their highway to where river and ocean meet, at last.

Elizabeth Bogutt

how long

Daylight's rolling in
Like a blemished star
With its twinkle tucked away
In a dark valley
Where its aroma
Once fluttered in the wind
Like a fancy feather
Where its mist
Once rippled in the sky
Like swirling satin

Now look how its freshness wanes-
Lulled to sleep
By the wails of the wolves
As they roam
Through barren forests
Once rich with the bounty of nature

How long will the sun
Blaze through the billowing clouds
Tarnished from human wear?

How long will the murmuring brook
Chase the glimmer of the sun's light
Into the dawn?

Noreen Inglesi

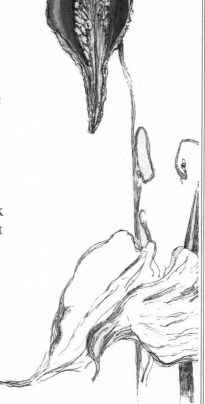

oh morning dove

Oh morning dove
Perched atop frozen housetops
Awaiting winter's tardy slumber
Longing to catch sight
Of the dandelions and tulips
In graceful arabesque with the wind
So anxious to take flight
Atop the green of the meadows
Whilst respiring the blended fragrance
Of the wildflowers and honeysuckles
Until eventide
When you can cast your shadow
Upon the sleepy-eyed moon
Lying in the mist
Still basking in the gentle dew
Of the morning

❀ *Noreen Inglesi*

at beavertail point

I find
all nature erotic,
you said.

Even rocks.

 It was the waves
that whispered in our ears
all day long,
the sun
that pressed,
warm,
then hot.
Breezes
tickled the down
at the back
of your neck,

 but rocks?

Yes,
pale orange cliffs
sheltered us from wind,
cupped winter sun,
made it easy
to lounge,
to kiss till
the tide came in.

Below us, unseen
because we could not
unlock eyes from each other,
rocks made pools
to hold anemones

and protected them from the waves
for those languid hours—
anemones
who would have sucked our fingers
into themselves
at the slightest touch.

Bobbing seals sent sidelong glances
from deep, wet eyes.

Above the cliffs,
the wind would make
our nipples erect.
But down below, the rocks surrounded
us and poured us their cup of sunlight,
our sustenance.

All good qualities in a lover.

 But all that
anthropomorphizing
dropped away
as will happen
with enough simple being

 —the rocks have time,
know stillness—

All nature,
all being, erotic:

an invitation
to connect,
an invitation
to enjoy.

※ *Karina Lutz*

Originally published in S/tick, 13.2 (Winter 2018): 14, 32.

matunuck hills preserve

Slopes steep and slippery
Slushy leaves moistened
With melted snow
Wind gently rustling
Through brittle branches

Paths twining, twisting,
Leading finally to
Soft soothing sunlight
Shaded with images
Of forsythia in early bloom
Glistening atop
An ice-capped kettle pond
Tucked safely away in Matunuck Hills

At water's edge
A cormorant swiftly swoops down
For its spoil
While a crane stretches its neck
And peers peacefully
At its own reflection

A few faint footprints
In the velvety snow
The only trace of man
In this wildlife refuge

Deer can wander here
In the untamed night
Far from the barrels of hunters
Far from the honking of horns
And the bustling
Of all night shoppers

Larva can lie
Dormant in its cocoon
Until spring
When it soars
As a damselfly
In the soft winds
Of the gentle sky
Amidst the pure fragrance
Of a freshly blooming rose

※ *Noreen Inglesi*

spring tide

Somewhere unseen the moon swings into line
with the sun, which springs the tide
that drives water high up the ramp
toward the dry skiff waiting
for cool liquid to lick its prow,
moisten its bottom,
loosen its grip on ground,
rock and dip it gently,
then lift and slip it
over wood and moss and seaweed
through a splash of marsh grass
onto the stirring surface of the world.

※ David Riley

*Previously published in 2006 in
Summer Lines, A Decade of
Tenants Harbor Poetry Readings*

quicksand pond

The blissful sun
Quivers atop
The swirling salted water
Slowly unveiling
The soft sand bottom
Of Quicksand Pond

A piping plover
Contentedly feasts there
On its muddy flats
So close to the dunes
And the breakers
Of Goosewing Beach

In the air
The unique aroma
Of a salty breeze
Whisking through
The pond's slender grasses
Resounding the image
Of this peaceful haven

❋ Noreen Inglesi

the nature conservancy on block Island

On a bright, cloudless day
You can discern with your naked eye
The delicate contour of Block Island
Whilst sauntering through
The speckled sands of Galilee
A mere boat ride away
From this 6400 acre island,
Fashioned by glaciers some 10,000 years ago
Its barrier beaches, ponds and thick shrubs
Provide a haven
To many of our state's most endangered species

From Elizabeth Dickens Trail,
A small bird peeks out
Through a sunny space in the thickets
Securely nestled, tucked away,
Nurtured in this habitat
Named for a special person,
A teacher of natural history
Who single handedly sparked
Community awareness for
Preserving the island's natural treasures

From its Clayhead Trail you may
Catch a glimpse of the migrating songbird
Feasting on its fruited shrubs
Sheltered in its southerly and northerly trek
Along the Atlantic Flyway

After entering the wooden gates of Rodman Hollow
You must pause and breath in the fresh scent of bayberry
It is here
Where the state-threatened Northern Harrier
Grazes and nests
It is here
That the Nature Conservancy on Block Island
Had its inception
Where Captain John Rob Lewis
Organized islanders to protect
Its natural habitats
It is here where many separate groups
Work as one

For, Block Island, is in essence
The epitome of a community pitching in
To make a positive difference

☀ Noreen Inglesi

seascape

My mother and I by the sea—
my wife on the bluff's edge etching
the wind-swept waves.
The sea is performing wild feats—
hoisting the ponderous weight of its dense green body
into air, and curling over the edge of the rock-strewn shore
to thunder down in splinters, coils, eddies—

"Look at that one!" we cry, and the green sea arches hugely
over itself, lunges, breaks, and the spume
leaps skyward, sides of rocks stream white,
and under our feet
the veined foam swishes, curls—

And the wind tugs at our clothes,
lashes hair
against our wind-burned faces,
salts our lips and eyes—
and for over an hour we sit watching the waves
arch up, crumble, sweep—
drenched in the fierce green power and
beauty of the sea.

Eighty times
the earth has circled the sun.
We may not come here again
We may not come here again

(My mother is old,
our mother, the sea, is old),
but sit here now
happy,
lost in the thunderous burstings of the sea.

My wife stands up and waves,
her picture done.

We climb the bluff,
stopping at each level niche
to breathe—
and at the top
look back.

Only the moon tonight
shall see that ancient, deep-troughed face unwrinkle
and turn as smooth as a child's.

✺ Paul Petrie

from his book, Rooms of Grace: New and Selected Poems,s
New Orleans Poetry Journal Press, 2005.

forms of violence

Five billion to zero was the final result
When every hunting game was over.
The firing of every gun that chafed in its holster
Lost its purpose
Once every passenger
Pigeon was squeezed out of sky
Targeted for extinction
By what we triggered.
Martha RIP 1914. She was the last.
It was an old story –
How someone's world always gets trampled somehow –
Condos going up, raised like rifles
Animals of all stripes going homeless
Forgotten stars bereft of their old shine
Unable to resurrect like weeds
Through their hard and vacant lots.
More land for us, more resources, more everything –
Less land, fewer resources, more empty hunting for them

Hungry for our understanding of their fight
Until they could no longer soldier on
Their dwindled army
Flagging to half-mast
With the killing
Until the flagpole clinked and clinked
Metallic as guns re-loading, aiming for imminent domain –
Every world, every marsh, every home standing in our way.
Stop, look around
Feel how the taken-for-granted breeze
Cool the heat of anger
Or how the palm trees
Speak sway dialect in a language –
How they can tell the storm to relax.
Be grateful for every animal that needs to survive
Teaches you about survival
And what you can't survive.
Load their hopes for your understanding.

✺ David Dragone

untitled

So Sonya asked me what winter feels like
and from the view of spring it feels like struggling to blossom through
the surface after the protection of season's sleep
It feels like moments before awakening to a sun weeks after it rises taller
and remembering you forgot that life was not all shadow
It feels like the solvency of the sight that showed the contrast without
squinting at energy so spectacular even in its subtlety
It feels like the buds of awareness, of discovery--
of recognizing that passion is vitality when our vitality depends on us
loving this earth enough to protect it.

What does winter feel like?
Does it feel like tundras, sprinkled with spring and hurricane season on
the northeast that no one thought was coming
They thought it was snow but the temp suddenly rose and those that
joked that this is the way it goes in New England were many
and although not a seat at the carbon pricing hearing was empty the bill
was tabled for further study after four years of being tabled for further
study
Not to propose that there could not be a better solution to the
frightening choices that harm our children and the children of tomorrow
Not to disclose that maybe, we're not reaching high enough.

It's not summer
but the blood in my veins is on fire and the water inside me is screaming
solutions to its subtly portrayed sacrificial recital
As if this is normal
As if it's not a crime to cage clean water for profit in a state that's been
poisoned by deadly exposures.
It feels like winter when
you forgot about the leaves that fell
the five dollars that you felt were good enough to help another town
fallen victim of a human corporate hell
Because corporations have rights as humans
and as such they take away human rights because we think contradictions

apparent in our own language are nothing but symbolic
That what is right is up to the law which is up for interpretation which
is plentiful and varied among those with a soul they're trying to sell
These leaves, a couple seeds that planted flowers since college but
these four years we've needed trees
We've needed green
We've needed energy with a cost that wouldn't exceed what we need to
sustain our life in all its beauty.

It feels like winter when
Another season of stories are exposed from snow and the plastic bags
come pouring
When it stays through spring's arrival to remind us that now we earn
our sleep if we want protect the songs of peace
Spring must be exploding with celebration of the movement that
competes against this time of grief
That can quote you the corruption and point fingers at the thieves
That isn't afraid of fables of defeat
That cries out when black snakes come to eat the very land from which
they feed
That stand together on the broken rope of leadership they were handed
and mend it stronger than you ever would believe
Spring is exploding with violent winds screaming for relief that will
only be provided if we roll up our sleeves and commit to the decree
that will take back what has been stripped by power hungry greed and
robbed us of ability to breathe.

We're taking back our right to be
Forests of tireless demands, no these are not pleas these are not naive
means of retrieving the justice that was so long betrayed by poison,
greed
We're cleaning up through humble means of coming together
Union is all we need
Sun rising
Natural light to set free minds dusted with centuries of lies and

disguises
Sun rising
Natural light to set free the right to walk safely into darkness
Sun rising
Natural light to bring back love on the horizon
Sun rising
No more climate compromises
We are fighting
We stop lifeless licensing the right to survival
Sun rising
Now's time to pay your prices
and to enforce it you better believe that I am not the only one that
is willing to die trying.

☀ Nicole DiPaolo

this tree

This tree stands
With wrinkled trunk
Its arms stretching
With ease
With even the gentlest
Of breeze

Its strong roots
Keep it tall and straight
Safe until the
The storms abate

This tree has lived through
Hazy heat and bitter frost
Has seen many days
Of summers lost

This tree which gives us
Breath, shelter and shade
Is quenched by even the
Tiniest moist drop made

This tree tells of the days
Gone by
And has seen more
Of life
Than you and I.

✾ Noreen Inglesi

untitled

Autumn sky
so high
above ....
don't you know I love to see your gray
luminescence permeating me and mine -
life, death, sickness, health
so intertwined.
Matter, molecules, atoms, particles – moving
so fast.
Is it real?
Will it last?
If I change my mind
Will I change time?
If I choose to feel
will it be real?
Who decides?

☀ Kelly Melear Hough

smokeless sky

Birds in flight clouds that are puffy and white sturdy tall
Oak trees that reach way up high in a SMOKELESS SKY
Today is a dark, dismal rainy day with too many cars in the way
Fresh air and sunshine we need to push the pollution away

The rivers the streams and forest creatures need to run free
We must respect why Mother Nature created you and me

Way up there an eagle soars autumn leaves begin to fall
On the ground as I walk by below the SMOKELESS SKY

Please do not hesitate to make a change about that pollution
Its waste left unattended in your local town litter so much
Hidden it can't be found

Junkyards that are filled with glass, metals things that rust
It is our civic duty to care about our planet...we must

The sun needs to shine she is our only true friend
One on whom we all must depend

For this world every generation and our nation should comply
Reason why we should live beneath a SMOKELESS SKY

❁ Amybeth Parravano

helping hands

Verse One

Goosewing Beach
With its nesting plovers
Volunteers keep a watchful eye
Pioneers for conservation
Saving land
Is their legacy

Refrain

Some have given acres
Some have given time
Helping hands
With one plan
Saving land
Helping hands with one plan
Protecting land

Verse 2

Land trusts
Save our open spaces
Special signs
Mark the sacred land
Soon we'll see
For a brighter future
Saving land
Is necessity

Refrain

Some have given acres
Some have given time
Helping hands with one plan
Saving land
Helping hands with one plan
Protecting land

☀ Noreen Inglesi

storm

Come......
The storm is always with us now
And visibility is poor, while
The world loses color,
While the gray rain blurs the lines between us
I would love to meet you
For one heartfelt honest moment
To stand together
Here,
Beside the unpaved roads of tomorrow
And listen beyond our human voice
To the Earth as she quietly turns away
And know it is time for us
To listen and decide

I would tell you
In these vague
Unraveling days of aftermath,
I have heard the wind speaking in tongues,
A presence as restless as fire,
As sad and certain as the sea
Trying to make contact,
Straining to invade my sleep,
Straining to pierce the glaze of small talk
And endless cups of coffee,
Pressing up against the tedious
Rooms of my daily life
Where I'm busy and working
And busy and tired....
And yet, and even then
It would still reach into my heart
With its troubling language
To summon me towards perception
As if to say....observe!
Beyond the momentums of your history!

Bleak of ghostlands of cities and forests,
Bleak with the trillion bitter choices
That have left us here
In the scorched air
And rusted meadows
Where thinning creatures come to bathe
Amidst the dying light

Have you wrestled with this too?
And somehow known
It was time for massive change,
Time for us to empty our pockets
Of all the angry coins
Revenge and more,
Politics and greed
And stand outside the storyline
That holds us hostage,
Free to jettison its toxic prizes
And frantic hardware,
Free to stand simply again
United, still,
To fathom the enormity of who we truly are
And what we may have lost

I would go with you then
Out beyond the graveyards
Of the lost cities
To pause with you,
Pause and look up
Up past skylines and fitful air
Up where the unfinished night
Twists against the sky,
Where the stars,
Like dice,
Are hurled
Against the mystery
And miracles are born
And squandered

And know
It is time for all the world
To stand together and feel the universe
Unfolding all around
And hear the streaming fingertips
Of light calling out
From galaxies far away
For us to look!
And be aware
That the great curvature of forces
Stands poised in fragile balance
Awaiting our decision
To listen and decide

In this time of rain
When seasons seem disfigured
The wind is loud and unrelenting,
Come from mountains
Come from mystery
Spreading out
Through star-struck sleepless nights
To prowl against our hearts
To speak to us in dreams
And wake us from this deadly sleep

The long arc of consequence
Has finally arrived
And chosen us
To be the final word
The last defense
To kneel down beside this wounded miracle
To listen and befriend

For the Earth is turning,
Turning back
Towards the terrifying beauty of creation
Where she was born
Where all is still

And she will turn away from us forever
Unless we can decide,
Here! Now!
With our backs against the void
To begin again
With courage and with love
To undo what has been done

So come...
Come as close as you dare
And let us go together

The storm is always with us now
And the visibility is poor

This is the time for vision
And there are those
Who do not see

※ Thomas Lane

rise up

Verse One
They say that global warming
Is just a normal trend.
They don't believe what science says
They think it's in their heads.
Just take a look around us
And analyze what's said
Our mother earth's in trouble
And we could wind up dead.

Refrain
Rise up rise up
Together we are strong
Let us use our voices
Let them feel our storm
Rise up rise up
People hand in hand
Together we can make a mark
Once we take a stand.

Verse 2
The polar caps are melting
Right before our eyes.
The polar bears can't stay afloat
Will lead to their demise.
Stronger floods and hurricanes
Rising tides and winds
Historic and destructive
What future will we give?

Refrain
Rise up rise up
Together we are strong
Let us use our voices
Let them feel our storm.
Rise up rise up people hand in hand
Together we can make a mark
Once we take a stand.

Verse 3
The seas are arising
There's no time to waste
The EPA has taken back
The progress that we made
Energy efficiency
Paris talks all gone
They're building endless pipelines
Right where they don't belong.

Refrain
Rise up rise up
Together we are strong
Let us use our voices
Let them feel our storm
Rise up rise up
People hand in hand
Together we can make a mark
Once we take a stand.
Together make them understand

✳ Noreen Inglesi

tomorrow

Like a starfish
Tucked safely in the soft sands
Lying there amidst summer's mirth
There's a star
Hidden inside all of us
Longing for us
To take the time
To feel its touch
And to nurture
Its iridescent glow
Like fireflies
We long to
Synchronize our flicker
Into one vibrant flare
Radiating boundlessly
In the gentle breeze of tomorrow

☀ Noreen Inglesi

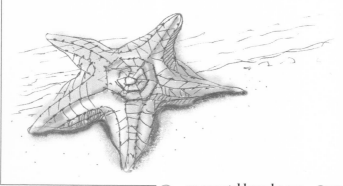

environmental agencies

American Lung Association in Rhode Island
Our mission is to save lives by improving lung health and
preventing lung disease. Our vision is a world free of lung
disease. Our strategic imperatives are to defeat lung cancer,
to improve the air we breath so it will not cause or worsen lung
disease, to reduce the burden of lung disease on individuals
and their families, to eliminate tobacco use and tobacco-
related diseases and to accelerate fundraising and enhance
organizational effectiveness to support the urgency of our
mission.

> 260 West Exchange Street
> Suite 102B
> Providence, Rhode Island 02903
> Lung Helpline: 1-(800)-lung-usa
> Phone: (401) 533-5179
> Website: www.lung.org
> Contact: Jennifer Wall
> E-mail: Jennifer.Wall@lung.org

Appalachian Mountain Club
The goal of the AMC is to promote the protection, enjoyment
and wise use of the mountains, river and trails of the Northeast.

> 130 Sudbury Street
> Providence, Rhode Island   02908
> Phone: (401) 351-2234
> Website: www.outdoors.org
> Contact: Linda Pease
> Email: linda.pease@cox.net

> Volunteer Opportunities:
> Clear and cleanup trails.

Blackstone River Watershed Council
To restore, enhance and preserve the physical, historical and cultural integrity of the Blackstone River, its watershed and its eco-system, through public advocacy, education, recreation, stewardship and the promotion of our unique Blackstone Valley resource.

Mailing Address:
P.O. Box 8068
Cumberland, Rhode Island 02864
Phone: (401) 723-8828
Website: www.blackstoneriver.org
Contact: Judy Hadley
Email: BRWCFOB@gmail.com

Blackstone Valley Tourism Council
To inspire and increase sustainable tourism in the Blackstone River Valley.

175 Main Street
Pawtucket, Rhode Island 02860
Phone: (401) 724-2200
Website: www.blackstonevalleytourismcouncil.org
Email: info@tourblackstone.com
Contact: Donna Kaehler
Email: keep@tourblackstone.com

Volunteer Opportunities:
To keep Blackstone Valley beautiful.

Childhood Lead Action Project
The Childhood Lead Action Project's goal is to eliminate childhood lead poisoning through education, parent support and advocacy.

> 1192 Westminster Street
> Providence, Rhode Island 02909
> Phone: (401) 785-1310
> Website: www.leadsafekids.org
> Contact: Laura Brion
> Email: info@leadsafekids.org

> Volunteer opportunities: Advocacy and outreach

Climate Action RI
The increasing destabilization of Earth's climate due to fossil-fuel combustion is a scientific fact and a threat to our collective well-being. In light of this threat, our Organization's mission is to change the way our society creates and uses energy, focusing on the elimination of fossil fuel extraction and use, and the way we work together in anticipation of climate change. We do this work through vivid, nonviolent actions that stimulate public engagement; direct communication with stakeholders and legislators; and mutual support with other organizations whose missions overlap our own. We are committed to climate and environmental justice across all sectors to foster a healthy and equitable society.

> Phone: (401) 440-0665
> Website: world.350.org/rhodeisland/
> Contact: Nicole DiPaolo
> Email: nicolelenadipaolo@gmail.com

Volunteer opportunities:
Include making art, knocking on doors, lobbying legislators and coordinating and participating in big events.

Environmental Justice League of Rhode Island

To promote safe and healthy environments for all by building power, leadership and action in the communities most affected by environmental burdens. EJLRI envisions a Rhode Island where we all have a healthy place to live, work and play regardless of race, ethnicity, or income.

    1192 Westminster Street
    Providence, Rhode Island   02909
    Phone: (401) 383-7441
    Website: www.ejlri.org
    Contact: Steve Roberts, Organizing Director
    Email: steve@ejlri.org

Filarski/Architecture + Planning + Research

We are an integrated architecture, design and planning, ecology studio and research workshop. The studio has been recognized with national, regional, state, and local awards in architecture, planning, urban design, and sustainable building/ecological systems research from professional societies, government agencies and citizen organizations. The studio and workshop is dedicated to innovation and excellence in design and planning creating a working landscape of ecology directed toward social responsibility and stewardship, lifelong learning, sustainable and renewable environments, and appropriate technology and economics in our urban, rural, coastal, corporate, and ecological communities.

    Mailing Address:
    PO Box 3210
    Providence, RI 02909
    Phone: (401) 331-8800
    Contact: Ken Filarski
    Email: kjfilarski@yahoo.com

    Volunteer opportunities: Grant work, etc.

Friends of Blackstone River Environmental Center

    100 New River Road
    Manville, Rhode Island 02838
    Contact: Keith Hainley
    Phone: (401) 996-1542

    Volunteer opportunities: Clean up and evasive plant control.

Green Circle Design
Sustainable landscape architecture.

> 286 Rochambeau Avenue
> Providence, Rhode Island 02906
> Phone: (401) 421-9599 or (401) 996-4922
> Website: www.Greencircledesign.net
> Contact: Kate Lacouture
> Email: kate@greencircledesign.net

Green Energy Consumers Alliance
We enable everyday people to make green energy choices in the most cost-effective, practical and seamless ways possible, and to advocate for energy policies that benefit the greater good.

> 2 Regency Plaza, Suite 8
> Providence, Rhode Island 02903
> Phone: (401) 861-6111
> Website: www.greenenergyconsumers.org
> Contact: Priscilla De La Cruz
> Email: Priscilla@greenenergyconsumers.org

Volunteer opportunities: part-time interns.

Greene School (The)
The Greene School explores the interdependence of human and natural systems. Through a rigorous pre-college curriculum, we develop citizens and leaders engaged in finding peaceful and sustainable solutions to local and global challenges. We are located on 70 acres of natural forest in West Greenwich, Rhode Island.

> 94 John Potter Road, Unit 3
> West Greenwich, Rhode Island 02817
> Phone: (401) 397-8600
> Website: www.tgsri.org
> Contact: Joshua Laplante, Head of School
> Email: jlaplante@thegreeneschool.org

Institute at Brown for Environment and Society (IBES)

With a changing climate and growing population, our fragile planet is at risk. Today's complex global changes call for innovative thinking. Business as usual is no longer effective. To work toward an equitable and sustainable future, Brown University launched the Institute for Environment and Society (IBES) in 2014. An education and research hub, IBES harnesses academic excellence from many disciplines, including climatology, sociology, ecology and economics. At this dynamic cross-campus center, students and faculty collaborate to discover, teach and learn at the crossroads of human aspirations and the environment that sustains us. Through a spirit of open collaboration, IBES is singularly poised to provide a concrete knowledge basis for informed decisions and to impact real-world policies.

Mailing Address:
Box 1951, 85 Waterman Street
Providence, Rhode Island 02912
Phone: (401) 863-3449
Website: brown.edu/environment
Email: environment@brown.edu

Listening Tree Cooperative

Listening Tree Coop is a community of equality- and ecology-minded individuals, sharing meals, permaculture farming, hosting community events, and living cooperatively together in Chepachet, RI. We are a cooperative household, incorporated as a limited equity housing cooperative to preserve farmland for farming, housing for people, and make it permanently affordable to do both here.

87 Reservoir Road
Chepachet, Rhode Island 02814
Phone: (401) 710-9784
Website: listeningtree.coop
Contact: Karina Lutz
Email: karinalutz@hotmail.com

Volunteer Opportunities:
Interns for organic farming

Mercy Ecology

Our mission is to instill reverence for Earth and to work towards sustainability of life by acting in harmony with all creation.

> 75 Wrentham Road
> Cumberland, Rhode Island   02864-1124
> Website: www.mercyecology.org
> Email: newdawn@mercynortheast.org

Nature's Trust RI

Nature's Trust RI is a youth-centered campaign to protect and enforce the legal right to a healthy climate for present and future generations.

> 52 Nichols Road
> Kingston, RI 02881
> Phone: (401) 871-1289
> Website: naturestrustri.org
> Facebook: www.facebook.com/NaturesTrustRI/
> Email: NaturesTrustRI@pobox.com

Statements from our Youth can be found at http://naturestrustri.org/youth-and-young-adults-speak-out-2/

Notable Works Publication and Distribution Co., Inc.

A non-profit arts organization dedicated to raising awareness for environmental and social issues through the arts.

> Mailing Address:
> PO Box 8122
> Cranston, Rhode Island   02920
> Phone: (401) 585-4037
> Website: www.notableworks.org
> Contact: Bina Gehres
> Email: binagehres@cox.net

> Volunteer Opportunities:
> Assist with projects and events.

Protect Rhode Island Brook Trout

The establishment of Protect RI Brook Trout was motivated by a powerful interest in preserving, protecting, and restoring wild brook trout populations in Rhode Island. As concerned citizens, our goal is to advocate for ecologically-based management and enhanced conservation efforts for this state's only remaining wild and native salmonid.

Pond Meadow Drive
Charlestown, Rhode Island 02813
Website: www.protectribrooktrout.org
Contact: Brian O'Connor
Email: oconnobri@gmail.com

RI Association of Railroad Passengers

The RI Association of Railroad Passengers' goal is to improve the rail transportation system in Rhode Island.

406 Stony Lane
North Kingstown, Rhode Island 02852
Phone: (401) 295-1311
Website: www.riarp.org
Contact: Everett Stuart
Email: evstuart@verizon.net

Volunteer opportunities:
Rail policy, operations and some work on the national level.

RI Committee on Occupational Safety and Health

Rhode Island Committee on Occupational Safety & Health (RICOSH) is Rhode Island's best resource for workplace safety, health and injury prevention training and information.

741 Westminister Street
Providence, Rhode Island 02903
Phone: (401) 751-2015
Website: www.facebook/RICOSH
Contact: Jim Celenza
Email: jascelenza@gmail.com

RI Interfaith Power and Light

As people of faith, we believe we all have a moral responsibility to protect the Earth's natural systems and to safeguard the well being of the most vulnerable to climate change, but least responsible for it- the poor of the world and future generations.

Mailing Address:
PO Box 15043
Riverside, Rhode Island 02915
Phone: (401) 324-9142
Website: www.ri-ipl.org
Contact: Katherine Gibson
Email: kmg4612@verizon.net

Sunrise RI

Sunrise is a movement to stop climate change and create millions of good jobs in the process. We're building an army of young people to make climate change an urgent priority across America, end the corrupting influence of fossil fuel executives on our politics, and elect leaders who stand up for the health and well-being of all people.

We are ordinary young people who are scared about what the climate crisis means for the people and places we love. We are gathering in classrooms, living rooms, and worship halls across the country. Everyone has a role to play. Public opinion is already with us - if we unite by the millions we can turn this into political power and reclaim our democracy.

Contact: Emma
Email: contact.riclimate@gmail.com
Website: facebook.com/SunriseRhodeIsland
Facebook: http://www.facebook/SunriseRhodeIsland/

Buckeye Brook Coalition

Protection and restoration of Buckeye Brook and its tributary streams and watershed.

Mailing Address:
PO Box. 9025
Warwick, Rhode Island   02889
Phone: (401) 739-6592
Website: www.buckeyebrook.org
Contact: Michael Zarum
Email: located@rcn.com

Volunteer opportunities:
Seasonal for fish count and clean up.
Contact: Paul Earnshaw
Email: brookeye10@gmail.com

Environmental Council of Rhode Island

We are a coalition of organizations and individuals. Our mission is to serve as an effective voice for developing and advocating policies and laws that protect and enhance Rhode Island's environment. We are proud of our long history of environmental advocacy dating back to 1972.

Mailing Address:
PO Box 9061
Providence, Rhode Island   02940
Phone: (401) 621-8048
Website: www.environmentcouncilri.org
Contact: Greg Gerritt
Email: environmentalcouncil@earthlink.net

Volunteer opportunities:
Seeking people to speak out on
legislation and policy at the Rhode Island state house.

Providential Gardener

Mission: Providential Gardener sees Rhode Island as a garden we all tend today so that future generations can enjoy living in this beautiful state. We focus on the question, Who does what to take care of Rhode Island? The website includes a comprehensive calendar of environment-related events (What Grows On in RI), a directory of organizations that take care of our environment, and news about RI's environment. All of this information is organized by more than 30 categories, including Climate.

Mailing Address:
PO Box 2556
Providence, RI 02906
Phone: 401) 273-6678
Website: www.provgardener.com
Contact: Susan Korte
Email: skorte@providentialgardener.com

Volunteer opportunities:
I could use volunteers to promote the calendar and website at tabling events and for entering events into the calendar through the Add Event form: https://www.provgardener. com/calendar/add-events

RI Bicycle Coalition

Our mission is to cultivate a physical and social environment in Rhode Island that encourages bicycling for all ages.

Mailing Address:
PO Box 2454
Providence, Rhode Island 02906
Phone: (401) 297-2153
Website: www.ribike.org
Contact: Sarah Mitchell
Email: info@ribike.org

Volunteer opportunities:
Volunteers needed for events.

RI Environmental Education Association

RIEEA is a network of professionals and organizations committed to promoting high-quality environmental education that increases the environmental literacy of all children and adults in our state. Our membership includes teachers, naturalists, environmental organizations, and educators from universities, recreation centers, and state, federal, and non-profit agencies, among many others. We foster collaborations, sponsor professional development opportunities, gather and disseminate information on environmental education, and promote public understanding of the value of an environmentally literate citizenry.

Mailing Address:
P.O. Box 40884
Providence, RI 02940
Website: rieea.org
Email: info@rieea.org

American Chestnut Foundation, The MA/RI Chapter of the

Dedicated to restoring the keystone forest tree of the east by breeding local American chestnut "Mother" trees into a population of blight-resistant trees.

> 209 Richardson Street
> Oxbridge, MA 01569-1621
> Phone: (508) 278-3565
> Website: www.acf.org
> Contact: Yvonne Federowicz
> Email: Yvonne.federowitz@gmail.com

Aquidneck Island Land Trust

Our mission is to preserve and steward Aquidneck Island's open spaces for the lasting benefit of the community, while connecting people with the land that defines the Island's natural character.

> 790 Aquidneck Avenue
> Middletown, Rhode Island 02842
> Phone: (401) 849-2799 ext. 18
> Website: aquidnecklandtrust.org
> Contact: Laura Freedman Pedrick
> Email: lpedrick@ailt.org

> Volunteer opportunities:
> If people want to volunteer, they may go to this page
> on our web site and complete the form:
> https://ailt.org/ways-to-give/volunteer/

Audubon Society of Rhode Island

The purposes of the Audubon Society of RI are to foster conservation of wild birds and other animal and plant life; to conserve wildlife habitat and unique natural areas through acquisition or other means; to carry out a broad program of public conservation education; to focus public attention on natural resource problems; to provide leadership when action on natural resource problems is necessary, and to do all other things necessary to foster better management of the natural environment for the benefit of humans and all other life.

> 2 Sanderson Road
> Smithfield Rhode Island 02917
> Phone: (401) 949-5454
> Website: www.asri.org
> Contact: Celeste Donovan
> Email: cdonovan@asri.org
>
> Volunteer opportunities:
> Please check website.

Burrillville Conservation Commission

The Burrillville Conservation Commission's mission and goals are to protect and preserve the natural tranquility of the natural reserves, features and attributes that has defined the Town of Burrillville for over two hundred years.

> 105 Harrisville Main Street
> Harrisville, Rhode Island   02830
> Website: www.burrillville.org
> Contact: Richard Dionne
> Email: rdionne99@aol.com

Clean Ocean Access

The mission of Clean Ocean Access is to "take action today so future generations can continue to enjoy ocean activities." Our main programs are CLEAN (removing marine debris from the shorelines and changing human behavior to eliminate trash on the shoreline and in the ocean), OCEAN (permanent year round clean water on our shorelines) and ACCESS (make sure public access is and shoreline habitat is available and protected forever). We have a focus on Aquidneck Island and work off the island with partner organizations as required to achieve our goals.

> 23 Johnny Cake Hill
> Middletown, Rhode Island   02842
> Website: www.cleanoceanaccess.org
> Contact: Dave McLaughlin
> Email: dave.mclaughlin@cleanoceanaccess.org
>
> Volunteer opportunities:
> Listed on website.

Clean Water Action

The goals of Clean Water Action are clean, safe, and affordable water, clean up of toxic waste and aiding in the solid waste crisis of composting and recycling in market development.

> 60 Valley Street
> Providence, Rhode Island 02909
> Website: www.cleanwateraction.org
> Contact: John Berard
> Email: jberard@cleanwater.org

Common Fence Point Improvement Association

The Common Fence Point Improvement Association was formed to protect and maintain property and buildings held in trust including beaches, right of ways, playgrounds and salt marshes.

> 933 Anthony Road
> Portsmouth, Rhode Island   02871
> Website: www.commonfencepoint.org
>
> Volunteer opportunities:
> Help with events

Grow Smart

Grow Smart Rhode Island provides statewide leadership for diverse public and private interests seeking sustainable and equitable economic growth. We promote such growth by advocating for compact development in revitalized urban, town, and village centers balanced with responsible stewardship of our region's natural assets – farmland, forests, the coastline, and the Bay. We inform leaders, decision makers, and concerned citizens about the many benefits of compact development and asset stewardship and provide research and training on proven smart growth strategies. We convene broad coalitions that advocate policy reforms and specific projects designed to build communities where all people and businesses can thrive.

1 Empire Street # 523
Providence, Rhode Island 02903
Phone: (401) 273-5711
Website: www.growsmartri.org
Contact: Scott Wolf
Email: swolf@growsmartri.org

Deputy Director: John Flaherty
Email: jflaherty@growsmartri.org

Volunteer opportunities:
Assisting in policy research, data base updating, event support.

Groundwork Rhode Island

Our mission is to reconnect the fabric of urban communities by meeting the dual needs of environmental sustainability and economic prosperity in partnership with community residents, businesses, and other partners.

1005 Main Street, #1223
Pawtucket, Rhode Island 02860
Phone: (401) 305-7174
Website: www.groundworkri.org
Contact: Amelia Rose
Email: arose@groundworkri.org

Narragansett Bay Estuary Program

Our mission is to protect, restore, and preserve Narragansett Bay and its watershed.

The Narragansett Bay watershed is over 1 million acres in area and is home to almost 2 million residents from Rhode Island and Massachusetts. We collaborate with organizations from both RI and MA who work to protect wildlife, ensure water is safe and clean, and promote community involvement.

235 Promenade Street, Suite 393
Providence, Rhode Island 02908
Phone: (401) 633-0550
Website: www.nbep.org
Email: info@nbep.org
Contact;   julia.bancroft@nbep.org

RI Land Trust Council

The Rhode Island Land Trust Council's purpose is to foster a sustainable land conservation movement in Rhode Island by supporting the missions and operations of land trusts and providing a forum for their effective cooperation. These land trusts seek to preserve open spaces, natural areas, scenic character, watersheds, drinking water sources, farmland, forests, historic sites, and shorelines that uniquely define our communities. Collectively, we are preserving the heritage of our state for future generations.

Mailing Address:
PO Box 633
Saunderstown, Rhode Island 02874
Phone: (401) 932-4667
Website: www.rilandtrusts.org
Contact: Rupert Friday
Email: rfriday@rilandtrusts.org

Volunteer opportunities:
Clear trails.

Save The Bay
The Mission of Save The Bay is to protect and improve
Narragansett Bay.

100 Save the Bay Drive
Providence, Rhode Island 02905
Phone: (401) 272-3540 Ext. 119
Website: www.savebay.org
Contact: Topher Hamblett
Email: thamblett@savebay.org

Volunteer opportunities: Interns and volunteers
Email: volunteer@savebay.org

Sierra Club of RI
The Sierra Club of RI's goal is to preserve, enjoy, and protect our
environmental resources.

118 Gano Street
Providence, Rhode Island 02906
Website: www.sierraclub.org
Contact: Aaron Jaenig
Email: chair@risierraclub.org

South Side Community Land Trust
Southside Community Land Trust provides access to land,
education and other resources so people in Greater Providence
can grow food in environmentally sustainable ways and create
community food systems where locally produced, affordable, and
healthy food is available to all.

109 Somerset Street
Providence, Rhode Island 02907
Phone: (401) 273-9419
Website: southsideclt.org
Contact: Margaret De Vos
Email: margaret@southsideclt.org

Volunteer opportuinities: Farm work
Contact: Agnieszka

The Nature Conservancy (Rhode Island)

The Nature Conservancy of RI is part of an international non-profit organization with a single goal: Preserving rare and endangered species through the protection of the ecosystems that sustain them. More than 4,000 acres of RI land have been protected by the Conservancy since the early 1960's.

159 Waterman Street, Providence, RI 02906
Phone: (401) 331-7110
Website: www.nature.org
Contact: John Torgan
Email: jtorgan@tnc.org

West Bay Land Trust

The Mission of The West Bay Land Trust is to maintain a rich blend of wetlands, woodlands, urban preservation and pastoral space in the city of Cranston. Our goals include sustaining the working farms in the rural, western area of the city, as well as preserving the diverse nature of all Cranston's communities, thus allowing the city to offer a continued variety of residential lifestyles to its citizens.

Mailing Address:
PO Box 2205
Cranston, Rhode Island 02905
Website: www.westbaylandtrust.org
Contact: Lynne Harrington
Email: lynneharri@hotmail.com

Westerly Land Trust

The Westerly Land Trust, a not-for-profit corporation, operates throughout the town to preserve and enhance Westerly's sense of place. The Trust works to preserve open space, rehabilitate and renew older neighborhoods, and create educational and recreational opportunities for the public. Our programs and activities are designed to enhance our town's urban landscape as well as its natural environment, wildlife habitats, native plants, and water resources.

Mailing Address:
PO Box 601
Westerly, Rhode Island 02891
Phone: (401) 315-2610
Website: www.westerlylandtrust.org

Volunteer opportunities:
Trail maintenance, event volunteers, community gardening work, urban co-op and farmers' market.
Contact: Meg Lee

Wood-Pawcatuck Watershed Association

WPWA's goal is to ensure protection of the natural and historic areas of the watershed. Activities include: the River Captain Program and the Watershed Watch Program to build a base of information from visual observation of changes and weekly analysis of samples, the Pawcatuck Estuary Planning Project, an Environmental Fair for schoolchildren, clean-ups, canoe trips, and public forums.

203 Arcadia Road
Hope Valley, Rhode Island 02832
Phone: (401) 539-9017
Website: www.wpwa.org
Contact: Chris Fox
Email: chris@wpwa.org

Woonasquatucket River Watershed Council

In 1998 the Woonasquatucket River was designated as one of fourteen American Heritage Rivers. This federal designation honors the historic, cultural, economic and environmental significance of this Rhode Island treasure. The Woonasquatucket River Watershed Council (WRWC) protects and restores the urban river, as well as park spaces and a bike path directly alongside the river. WRWC runs many programs – Clean Days on the Greenway volunteer events, water and fish monitoring, bike and education lessons and activities, recreation events and more.

> 45 Eagle Street, Suite 202
> Providence, Rhode Island 02909
> Phone: (401) 861-9046
> Website: www.wrwc.org
> Contact: Alicia Lehrer
> Email: alehrer@wrwc.org

> Volunteer opportunities:
> Seeking help with clean up efforts.

Environmental Protection Agency (EPA) in Rhode Island

27 Tarzwell Drive
Narragansett, Rhode Island 02882
Phone: (401) 782-3000
Website: www.epa.gov/ri

Rhode Island Department of Environmental Management

The Rhode Island Department of Environmental Management (DEM) serves as the chief steward of the state's natural resources – from beautiful Narragansett Bay to our local waters and green spaces to the air we breathe. Our mission put simply is to protect, restore, and promote our environment to ensure Rhode Island remains a wonderful place to live, visit, and raise a family. We protect these precious resources through development and enforcement of environmental laws, and we strive to provide guidance to our many customers in complying with these laws.

We work with our partners to restore our lands and waters, to conserve wildlife and marine resources, and to monitor environmental quality so we can build healthy, more resilient communities.

We promote our natural resources – from our historic parks and beaches to our farms and delicious local food and seafood. We are focused on helping our state grow "green" and build desirable neighborhoods that offer ample space to recreate and connect with nature.

235 Promenade Street
Providence, Rhode Island 02908
Phone: (401) 222-4700
Website: www.dem.ri.gov